FOLENS HISTORY

BRITAIN 1750—1900

CONTENTS

Unit	Theme	Page
1.	Revolution in Farming	3
2.	Seaborne Empire	7
3.	Industrial Beginnings	9
4.	Development of Industrial Towns	11
5.	Steam Power	13
6.	Textile Industries	14
7.	Coal Mining	16
8.	Working in the Iron and Steel Industry	17
9.	Women in the Industrial Revolution	18
10.	Transport and Communications	20
11.	Anglicans and Methodists	23
12.	The Effects of the French Wars	25
13.	Corn Laws and Free Trade	27
14.	Radio Manchester 1819	29
15.	The Growth of Trade Unions	32
16.	The Great Exhibition of 1851	34
17.	Political Reform for Women	36
18.	Factory and Mine Reform	39
19.	Cholera and Public Health	40
20.	Medicine	42
21.	Education	43
22.	Heart of the Empire	46
	The National Curriculum	48

RESOURCE BOOK

RICHARD ALLISON
CAROLE BROWN

INTRODUCTION

This teacher-resource book is designed to support and extend *Britain 1750-1900*, the fourth of Folens' core text books which fulfil all the Attainment Targets of the National Curriculum Key Stage 3 History.

All Folens' history books aim to help pupils study history through the use and interpretation of evidence. Pupils are encouraged to examine primary and secondary evidence and to put together their own ideas about what might have happened.

Activities create opportunities for:

● the development of the ability to describe and explain historical change and cause, and analyse different features of historical situations;
● the development of the ability to understand interpretation of history;
● the development of pupils' ability to acquire evidence from historical sources and form judgements about their reliability and value.

Such activities relate directly to the three Attainment Targets set out for National Curriculum history. In addition a matrix is included at the end of this book in order that teachers may identify which Attainment Targets are being met by each unit.

The majority of units in this resource book can be photocopied for use in the classroom. They are designed to encourage the active involvement of pupils in the study of history. It is also hoped that at a time when 'paper pushing' threatens to take over, teachers will find these units ease the load of lesson preparation.

Note to teachers: The solutions to the exercise in Unit 2 are on page 48.

Acknowledgements

The authors and publishers would like to thank the Hulton Picture Library for permission to reproduce the photograph on page 25.

Illustrators:
Peter Dennis, Keith Howard, Lorna Turpin.

First published 1992 by Folens Limited, Albert House, Apex Business Centre, Boscombe Road, Dunstable LU5 4RL, England.

ISBN 1 85276125-3

Printed by Ashford Colour Press.

1. REVOLUTION IN FARMING

Aim

To consider the attitudes and circumstances of villagers involved in enclosure. To look at the changes in farming methods.

Introduction

Pupils can investigate different points of view through role play. The effect of enclosure on a village was enormous. By looking at it from different perspectives, pupils can understand its significance for both the community and the whole nation. Subsequently, we can attempt to understand how our interpretation of these events nowadays is based on this general picture and our knowledge of later developments.

Resources

Photocopiable resource sheets (pages 4, 5 and 6) giving information about the role play and two plans: the village before enclosure, and an outline to be filled in by each pupil, according to the outcome of the exercise.

Objective: for pupils to represent the viewpoint of families involved in enclosure.
Skill: analysis, selection, cooperation and communication.

Organisation

Pupils need to be arranged in 13 small groups of two or three.

Approach

▼ Pupils draw lots to identify which of 13 characters or families they will represent.
▼ They prepare their case for the meeting, discussing the prospects for their family if enclosure goes ahead.
▼ Some groups may decide to work together. For example, the Squire, Farmer Tracy and the Rector might collude. The families might also wish to cooperate or at least share their concerns or hopes about the outcome.
▼ The meeting is held with the Squire in the Chair.
▼ The local constable on the door ensures outsiders do not enter.
▼ Each group speaks once. Then a vote is taken. (This is an anachronism. However, it could have been used to draw proceedings to an end, and give all the villagers the impression that their interests were being considered. Pupils will realise that the decision depended on the size of each family's property, not the number of landowners.)

Debrief

Was the outcome inevitable? How far did our knowledge of the spread of enclosures influence our part in the role play?

Follow-up

Pupils can go on to take a general view of the situation by completing the plan of the village after enclosure.

REVOLUTION IN FARMING

How a Village was Enclosed

We are living in an English village in 1792. There is a growing demand for food in the towns and our village is not producing enough to bring profits to the larger farmers. Two landowners in particular, Squire Matthews and Farmer Tracy, are anxious to enclose the three open fields in which every family has strips, plus the common land, and make them separate farms for growing cash crops. They can then use fertilisers and new machinery more efficiently.

There are ten smaller freeholders and their families: the James, the Greens, the Blacketts, the Coates, the Harrisons, the two Dodgson families, and the three Williams families.

READ The following information.

Each family owns five strips. The Squire owns 35, Farmer Tracy 25 and the Rector, the Rev. Pargeter, has 12. Also in the village there is a blacksmith who has a few cattle which graze on the common and four families of squatters who have homes on the edge of the common but have no legal rights to their land.

Squire Matthews

He owns some of the best strips in each field and has most livestock on the common. He built his mansion ten years ago by the North Field. He is very keen to introduce crop rotation, new seed drills, ploughs and selective breeding to improve his cattle and sheep. His friends include big landowners and MPs who have told him how enclosing can raise efficiency and improve profits. As the local JP and biggest landowner in the village, he has the respect of most of the villagers.

Reverend Pargeter

He has a wife and daughter to support out of his small stipend and poorly farmed strips. He has to cooperate with the squire who appointed him to this parish, so he supports enclosure even though he cannot afford to spend much on improving his farming methods. He employs some poor labourers to work on his land.

Farmer Tracy

He is concentrating on livestock because of the growing market for fresh meat in the towns. He has already fenced off some of his own strips and part of the common to prevent his cattle mixing with other villagers' animals. He has sown turnips and clover on his own strips for fodder.

The Green, Coates and three Williams families

They are all progressive farmers who support enclosure. They plan to combine their strips to form neighbouring farms. Then they will cooperate to buy machinery, better livestock and fertilisers. Widow Mary Williams' son will soon be marrying the Greens' daughter. This may lead to a combination of the two farms later on.

The Blackett, Harrison, James and the two Dodgson families

The Blacketts, Harrisons, James and the two Dodgson families have not tried to improve their methods but concentrated on producing enough food for their own large families. However, the James and the Harrisons have fallen on hard times as the crops have failed and their livestock has declined through inter-breeding with weaker animals. Some of their children have had to go into the workhouse. Farmer James in particular feels ashamed but cannot see how he can pay off his debts and improve his farm to make a profit out of enclosure. Two of his cousins are squatters on the common.

REVOLUTION IN FARMING

The Roles

- Form 13 small groups (pairs or threes).
- Draw lots to decide which of the following roles you will play:

1. Squire Matthews
2. Farmer Tracy
3. Reverend Pargeter
4. James family
5. Green family
6. Blackett family
7. Coates family
8. Harrison family
9. Dodgson family (1)
10. Dodgson family (2)
11. Williams family (1)
12. Williams family (2)
13. Williams family (3)

- Think about what will happen to your family if the enclosure goes ahead.
- Prepare your arguments for the meeting.

The Village Meeting

Squire Matthews has called the meeting at his mansion to discuss the proposal to enclose all the village land. He needs to have the support of the owners of 80% of the land before a petition can be sent to Parliament for an Act of Enclosure. Farmer Tracy and the Rector support him. How many other freeholders does he need to win over to his point of view?

The squatters are not invited to the meeting. However, they are all related to some of the freeholders who have agreed to put forward their point of view at the meeting.

▼ The meeting begins with speeches by the Squire and Farmer Tracy.
▼ Then one of the freeholders who is against enclosure speaks.
▼ After that the discussion is open and finally the Rector urges everyone to make up their own mind.
▼ A vote is taken. What is the result?

The Enclosed Village

Sooner or later the Squire and his friends will get their way and the village will be enclosed.
- Complete the plan of the village after enclosure.
- Identify the areas which will be given to the freeholders by the Enclosure Commissioners who will redraw the map of the village.
- What will happen to the poorer freeholders? Will they sell their lands to the richer farmers and become labourers?
- What will happen to the squatters?
- Add a brief note explaining the effects of enclosure on the family you represented in the role play.

REVOLUTION IN FARMING

The village before enclosure

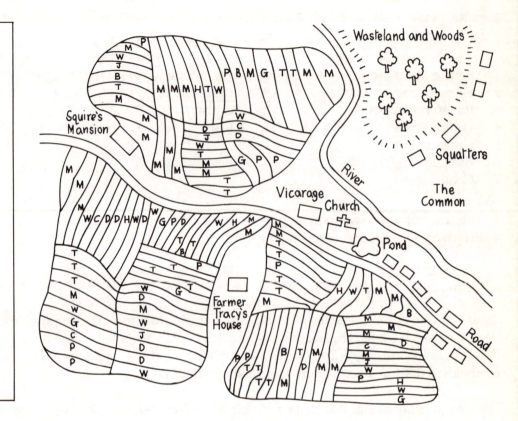

LAND
OWNERSHIP

M = Squire
Matthews
T = Farmer
Tracy
P = Rev. Pargeter
J = James
G = Greens
C = Coates
B = Blacketts
H = Harrisons
W = Williams
D = Dodgsons

The village after enclosure

LAND
OWNERSHIP

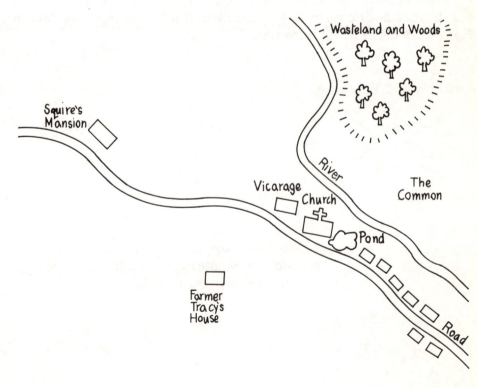

2. SEABORNE EMPIRE

READ The captions carefully and look at the pictures on the next page.

- Match the captions to the ships, and mount them on a series of cards.
- Place them in chronological order.
- What are the main changes you can see in the design of these ships?
- How far do these changes reflect the job each vessel was built for?
- What made the pattern of change more complicated?
- Did the age of sail end completely in 1900?
- How do we use large sailing ships today?

Captions

Tall-masted clippers such as the *Cutty Sark* brought the first crop of the Chinese tea harvest to Britain. The journey took less than 100 days. When the Suez Canal opened in 1869 steamships could make this journey far more quickly.

The East Indiamen resembled large Tudor galleons but they matched the fastest warships of the late 1700s. They carried passengers and 1 000 tons of cargo from India.

The first regular transatlantic steamship service was provided by the *City of Paris* in 1888. She had three funnels and sails were carried in case the engines broke down.

Brunel's *Great Eastern* was the biggest ship of her day. She was 680 feet long with six masts, five funnels, a screw propeller as well as paddle wheels. She was so big that she had to be launched sideways in 1858. However, many accidents and problems marred her voyages.

The first screw-driven (underwater propeller) steamship was Brunel's *Great Britain*. She had one central funnel and was the first iron ship to cross the Atlantic, taking 14 days to reach New York in 1845.

In 1840 the Canadian, Samuel Cunard, began the first regular transatlantic passenger and mail service using paddle steamers. The *Britannia* was designed with three masts to supplement the paddles.

By 1850 all new warships for the Royal Navy had steam engines. Along the hulls of both iron and wood were banks of cannons, similar to those on Nelson's *Victory* at the turn of the century. To save coal they still used sail as much as possible.

In the 1890s tall ships were still faster than steamships. When Charles Parsons developed a steam turbine, the speed of steamships doubled to 34 knots. The *Turbinia*, his own steam yacht, was sailed at the naval review of 1897 to demonstrate his invention. It seemed that the age of sail was almost over.

SEABORNE EMPIRE

1

2

3

4

5

6

7

8

3. INDUSTRIAL BEGINNINGS

To practise your observation skills and learn to interpret what you see.

At the picture below. It shows an artist's reconstruction of a room in a weaver's home. The date is the late 1700s.

- Find a partner to work with.
- Describe everything you can see in the picture, starting from the top. Here are some questions to help you:
  - ▼ How would you describe the structures at the top of the picture?
  - ▼ What material are these structures made from?
  - ▼ How many men and women are in the picture?
  - ▼ Describe the clothes of the people.
  - ▼ How old are these people?
  - ▼ How might these people be related?
  - ▼ What equipment is being used?
  - ▼ How is the equipment powered?
    CLUE TO SUCCESS: is it steam, water, engine, foot or hand power?
  - ▼ What job is each person doing?
- Working with your partner, write out a description of everything you have talked about.
- How is this picture different to any of the rooms in your own home?

INDUSTRIAL BEGINNINGS

THINK ABOUT

How you can use your description to interpret the picture. This means using the picture to learn about people and life at that time.

- Read the questions in the box below.
- Write 'yes' or 'no' in the 'Answer' column.
- Explain your answer in the 'Supporting Evidence' column. The first answer is completed for you.
- List anything else you can learn from the picture, in the box marked 'Other ideas'.
- Remember, interpretation is only YOUR ideas. You would need to examine a great deal more visual and written evidence before you could claim that your ideas are factually correct.

Question	Answer	Supporting Evidence
Were people able to make machinery?	Yes	Because I can see looms and a spinning wheel in the picture.
Did people work in their own homes?		
Were people able to weave cloth?		
Did people keep sheep?		
Did men and women work together?		
Did all children go to school?		
Were working conditions cramped?		
Were some jobs only done by men?		
Machinery was hand powered.		
Other ideas.		

4. DEVELOPMENT OF INDUSTRIAL TOWNS

LOOK

At the census return on the next page. It is for Stockton Street in the town of Middlesbrough. In 1851 Middlesbrough was in the county of Yorkshire, although today it is in Cleveland.

Before 1830 Middlesbrough was a small agricultural community. However, the land was bought by six men with a plan to develop the area as a port for the shipment of coal. This led to the development of a new town with heavy industry. In 1821 Middlesbrough had a population of 40, by 1851 it had reached 7 631. By 1901 it was 91 302.

The houses to which this census return refers were built with one room downstairs and one room upstairs. Toilets and tap water were outside and each one served several households.

Census returns are important pieces of historical evidence because they give us a great deal of information about life at the time.

NOW

1. Working with a friend, read the *CLUE TO SUCCESS* section and then go through the census return carefully.
   - How many houses are shown on this return?
   - To which street does this census refer?
   - Look at the ages of the people. Why do you think most people are fairly young?
   - Using the 'Occupations' column, what can you learn about industry in Middlesbrough in 1851?
   - What differences can you identify between the occupations of women and men?
   - Can you suggest at what age young people started working?
   - What do you notice about the widow Hannah Coates of number 6 Stockton Street, compared with other women whose status is wife?

2. Design a bar graph to show the number of people living in each house.
   - Can you draw any conclusions about the size of families in 1851?

3. Choose two or three families from the census and write a short report on each one.
   - Describe the family, giving their ages, occupations and place of birth.
   - If you subtract each person's age from the year 1851 you can find out in what year they were born.
   - Describe some problems which the family might have faced living in such accommodation.
   - Where husbands and wives were born a great distance apart, you might be able to suggest how they came to meet and marry.
   - Do any of the families seem to have moved around the country?

4. Draw up a family tree for the Wilkinson family.

CLUE TO SUCCESS:

Condition column	mar	= married
	un	= unmarried
Where Born column	DO	= ditto, which means 'as above'
Occupation column	Scholar	= a school pupil
	Pauper	= someone who has no income
	Shipwright	= a ship builder or carpenter
	Mariner	= a sailor

DEVELOPMENT OF INDUSTRIAL TOWNS

No. of House	Name of Street or No. of House	Name and Surname of each person who abode in the house on the night of 30th March, 1851	Relation to Head of Family	Condition	Age of Males	Age of Females	Rank, Profession or Occupation	Where Born	Whether Blind or Deaf and Dumb
1	Stockton Street	Ralph Bonn	Head	Mar	32		Shipwright	Yorkshire, Whitby	
	DO DO	Hannah Bonn	Wife	Mar		21		Yorkshire, Sandsend	
2	Stockton Street	John Pattison	Head	Mar	25		Mariner	Yorkshire, Sandsend	
	DO DO	Elizabeth Pattison	Wife	Mar		24		Yorkshire, Newbywiske	
3	Stockton Street	Sarah Goodall	Head	Mar		78	Pauper (farmer's wife)	Not known	
4	Stockton Street	William Wilkinson	Head	Mar	37		Seaman	Yorkshire, Whitby	
	DO DO	Mary Ann Wilkinson	Wife	Mar		36		Hampshire, Portsmouth	
	DO DO	Thomas James Wilkinson	Son	Un	13		Blacksmith Apprentice	Yorkshire, Middlesbrough	
	DO DO	William Wilkinson	Son	Un	11		Scholar	DO DO	
	DO DO	Dorthe Wilkinson	Daughter	Un		8	Scholar	DO DO	
	DO DO	Adam Wilkinson	Son	Un	3			DO DO	
	DO DO	Mary Ann Wilkinson	Daughter	Un		1		DO DO	
5	Stockton Street	John Liddle	Head	Mar	51		Iron Works Labourer	Durham, West Auckland	
	DO DO	Charlotte Liddle	Wife	Mar		56		Not known	
	DO DO	John Liddle	Son	Un	23		Tin Plate Worker	Kent, Deptford	
6	Stockton Street	Hannah Coates	Head	Widow		46	Butchery	Durham, Hilton	
	DO DO	Margaret Coates	Daughter	Un		20	Milliner	Durham, Stockton	
	DO DO	Sarah DO	DO	Un		16	Dressmaker	Yorkshire, Middlesbrough	
	DO DO	Hannah DO	DO	Un	13		Scholar	DO DO	
		Jane Calvert	Visitor	Mar		26		DO Catterick	

5. STEAM POWER

 **At the diagram below.**

Newcomen's steam pump

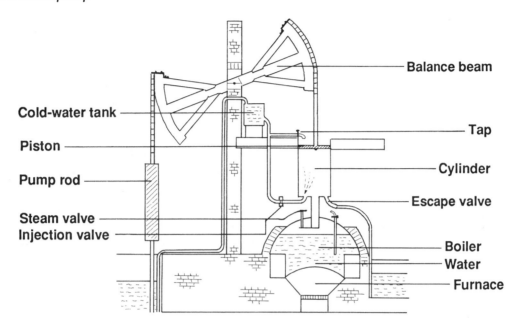

Although this engine used steam it was the atmospheric pressure which actually drove it. This is how it worked:

1. The steam valve opened.
2. The weight of the pump rod tilted the balance beam and the piston went up.
3. The cylinder filled with steam.
4. When the piston was as high as it would go, the steam valve closed.
5. The injection valve opened and cold water was sprayed into the cylinder. This condensed the steam and produced a vacuum, so that the air pressure pushed the piston down.

● Divide into pairs to explore how a steam engine worked.
● Make a copy of the diagram.
● Read the instructions explaining how the steam engine worked.
● Place the instructions face down on the table and using just the diagram, take it in turns to explain to each other how the steam engine worked.

Industries using steam engines by 1800

Cotton mills	84
Coal mines	30
Iron works	28
Copper mines	22
Canals	18
Breweries	12
Wool mills	9

● Display this information on a graph.
● How do you think steam engines might have been used in each of these industries?

6. TEXTILE INDUSTRIES

READ The following biography of Robert Owen 1771-1858.

Robert Owen was born the son of a Welsh saddler in 1771. He became apprenticed to a draper and soon showed exceptional business ability. When he was 20 Owen was managing a spinning mill.

During his early twenties, Owen married the daughter of David Dale, who owned large cotton mills in New Lanark in Scotland. By the time he was 29, Owen was controlling all his father-in-law's mills.

David Dale had built a special village to attract workers from Glasgow to his mill. Robert Owen took this a stage further as he believed the people who worked for him should be treated well. He improved their housing, reduced the number of hours they worked in the factory and increased their wages. He gave prizes to people who worked hard and began an old age pension scheme. He opened shops where prices were kept low. At first Owen's partners disagreed with many of his ideas, but as production and profits increased they changed their minds.

Owen refused to employ any child under the age of ten. Instead he provided them with free education, stopping all physical punishment. The children were taught basic subjects such as reading and mathematics, together with music and dancing. He employed about 11 teachers for 700 pupils.

Owen's model village was so successful that about 2000 people came each year to visit it. This pleased Owen, as he was eager for other employers to follow his example.

In 1816 he persuaded Parliament to look at the way factories were run. He hoped this would lead to a law stopping the employment of young children in cotton mills, and restricting the hours worked by adults. In 1819 Parliament did pass an Act to control the hours worked by children, but it was difficult to enforce. (See Unit 21 in the Core Text.)

Owen wanted more than just a model factory and village. He believed that people were only happy when they worked cooperatively, rather than competing. He set up a village of cooperation called New Harmony in America. Although the village was unsuccessful, Owen's ideas sparked off the formation of the cooperative movement which still exists today. His beliefs also laid the foundation for an early form of socialism.

On his return to England, Owen set up some basic labour exchanges. Here goods which had been made were exchanged. At first the scheme was very popular, but eventually it failed because only a limited variety of goods were brought to the exchange.

Owen also became involved with the Trade Union movement. In 1834 he persuaded many smaller unions to join together to form the Grand National Consolidated Trade Union. Although this union grew rapidly, it eventually collapsed owing to pressures from employers and the government. (See Unit 18 of the Core Text.)

- Using the dates given in this biography, draw up a time line showing the important events of Owen's life and work.
- Make a list of Owen's ideas which were new at that time.
- Can you identify any aspect of our life today which has been influenced by Robert Owen?
- Do you think Owen was an important individual? Explain your answer.

TEXTILE INDUSTRIES

READ — The following biography of Anthony Ashley Cooper, Lord Shaftesbury 1801-85.

Anthony Ashley Cooper was born into a very wealthy family. His father was the Earl of Shaftesbury and in 1851 Anthony inherited this title.

In 1826 Shaftesbury became a Member of Parliament. Following the Royal Commission of 1832, which investigated conditions in factories, Lord Shaftesbury became the leader of MPs who wanted to reform working conditions. He campaigned for many years in Parliament to pass laws improving the lot of working women and children. (Look at Unit 21 of the Core Text to find out more about these Acts.)

Lord Shaftesbury was dissatisfied with many of the Acts which were passed, but eventually in 1847, despite opposition from factory and mill owners, the Ten Hour Day Act was passed. This limited the working hours of young people and women. In 1878 the Factory Act gave greater protection to workers in all types of factories.

Shaftesbury was also concerned about people working in other industries, and in 1840 he set up a Parliamentary Commission to investigate mining conditions. When the report was published in 1842 people were very shocked and an Act was passed to improve working conditions. (See Unit 8 in the Core Text to learn more about mining.)

One group of workers which particularly concerned Shaftesbury were boy chimney sweeps. These boys often died from burns or suffocation while climbing chimneys to clean them. In 1864 Shaftesbury succeeded in persuading Parliament to pass an Act which forbade the use of children for this work.

However, it was not only working conditions which interested Shaftesbury. He helped to improve lunatic asylums where the mentally sick were chained down and treated like animals. He supported Florence Nightingale's work to improve hospital conditions and helped Dr Barnardo found a home for orphaned children.

Shaftesbury also took a great interest in education for the poor and for 40 years he was chairman of the Ragged School Union, which from 1844 provided free education for children of the very poorest people.

Although Shaftesbury felt great sympathy for the poor and worked constantly to improve their lives, he did not support political reform. In 1867 he voted against the Act which gave the vote to working men over the age of 21.

- Draw a spider diagram.
  - ▼ In the centre write Lord Shaftesbury's name and dates.
  - ▼ Give the spider five legs.
  - ▼ Place the following headings at the end of each leg:
    Factories
    Mines
    Children
    Medicine
    Education
- Using this biography write notes under each heading.
- Give examples of Shaftesbury's successes in helping the poor.
- Why do you think some people opposed his ideas about factory and mine reform?
- Why do you think Shaftesbury was against giving working men the vote?

7. COAL MINING

To reconstruct interviews with people from the past.

- Find a partner to work with.
- You will need paper for your notes.
- One of the pair will be the interviewer, the other the person being interviewed.
- Change over roles for the second interview.

Carefully at Unit 8 of the Core Text.

- Choose the role you want to play:
  Source A John Smith - *a trapper aged 8 years*
  Source C Betty Harris - *a mine worker*
- Read together the source you have chosen.
- The person playing the interviewer should prepare questions based on the source. The person being interviewed should read through the source several times.

CLUE TO SUCCESS:
This is an example of the sort of questions the interviewer might ask. (Source A is being used.)
1. How old are you?
2. Where do you work?
3. What sort of work do you do?
4. What sort of food do you take to work with you?
5. How many people do you work with?
6. What sort of light do you have?
- Working with your partner and using source A, see if you can answer these questions. Try out the questions and answers as if it was an interview.

- Look at the other source with your partner.
- Write out some questions similar to those above, but based on the second source.
- Complete two interviews and rehearse them carefully.
- Join another pair and comment on each other's interviews.

The reasons why women and children worked down the mines.

- Why might some women and children not want to be banned from working in the mines?

This page may be photocopied for classroom use only

8. WORKING IN THE IRON AND STEEL INDUSTRY

 **LOOK** At the picture below.

- Which industry are these people working in?
- Do mainly men or women seem to work in the industry?
- Write a few sentences about the working conditions. For example, do the people look hot or cold; comfortable or uncomfortable?
- What sort of accidents might have happened?

 **READ**

'The heat of the furnaces is terrible and the work most exhausting. The men have to wring their clothes when they go home. The work is unhealthy and dangerous. Disease carries the men off (kills them) at an early age. "The work affects you all over," said a worker to me. "You gets so cold that you shivers so you can't hold your food. The furnaces burn your insides out of you." This man had burns all over his body.'

Written by a reporter, Robert Sherard, in The White Slaves of England, *1897.*

 *NOW*

- Write down the name of the book this source is taken from.
- Who wrote the source?
- Why do you think the author wrote the source?
- Can you find anything in the picture above to support the sentence, 'The heat from the furnaces is terrible and the work is most exhausting.'?
- What do you think is the meaning of the sentence, 'The men have to wring their clothes when they go home.'?
- List some of the injuries and illnesses which the men suffered.
- Using the information from both the illustration and the written source, write a report about working in the iron and steel industry.
- From which source can you learn the most about working in the iron and steel industry?

9. WOMEN IN THE INDUSTRIAL REVOLUTION

 **LOOK** At the four pictures below. They show different methods of cooking.

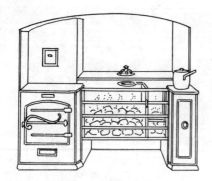

A

B

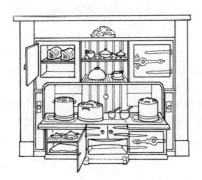

C

D

 **NOW**

- Put these pieces of cooking equipment in chronological order. Begin with the equipment which you think is the earliest.
- Explain why you think your answer is correct.
- Compare your answer with that printed upside down.

C *A kitchener or closed range of 1875. Notice that the fire is enclosed.*

D *A wood panelled gas cooker of c.1850. Very few people used these as they were thought to be smelly, noisy and dirty. By 1870 they had become popular with the wealthy.*

A *An open fire range of c.1850.*

B *An open hearth which was used for many centuries. Pots hung from a chimney crane. The meat was roasted on a spit.*

Both **A** and **C** were made from cast iron and needed to be polished with black lead everyday.

- On C, label: the four ovens, the grill, the hot plates for pans.
- On A, label: the oven which is to the left of the fire, the boiler for heating water to the right of the fire.
- What advantages did A have over B?
- What were the advantages of C?

WOMEN IN THE INDUSTRIAL REVOLUTION

Washing

For centuries washing had been done by rubbing clothes in water by hand. Gradually inventions were developed to help with this task.

In the early 1800s wooden washing machines were invented. The clothes were put in a wooden box which was then turned by a handle.

Morton's patent steam washing machine, 1844

In the early 1800s mangles were developed to wring water from clothes.

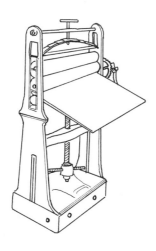

Tindell's Scotch mangle, 1850

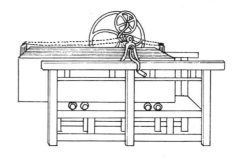

Box mangle, 1860

The box mangle was used by servants in most big houses. The clothes were wrapped around the wooden rollers and put under the large box which was filled with heavy stones.
● Why do you think two people were needed to operate this mangle?

● Explain what you think the advantages might have been for people who used these inventions.
● Do you think these inventions were used mainly by the poor or by the rich people?
● Give reasons for your answer.

After the First World War, equipment to help with washing developed rapidly. This was mainly because it became more difficult to employ people as servants.

10. TRANSPORT AND COMMUNICATIONS

Aim

To distinguish between different kinds and rates of change and to see how ideas and attitudes were affected.

Introduction

The period between 1750 and 1900 saw enormous developments in transport and communication. For the traveller, journey times across the country were reduced dramatically due to stage coaches and later the railways. Messages too could be received more quickly, by post and later by telegraph, telephone and radio. To understand the sequence and significance of these changes, the resource sheet identifies some major developments and inventions. It is worth remembering that an invention is often not immediately applied. It may take years before its value is recognised and it comes into general use. However, these changes affected everyone. They provided clear evidence that the 19th century was an age of progress and speed. The world would never be the same again.

Resources

Photocopiable resource sheet pages 21 and 22, and Unit 11 in the Core Text.

ACTIVITY

Objective: to consider the types and rates of change during the 19th century.
Skills: cooperative learning; drawing conclusions from different pieces of evidence.

Organisation

Pupils should work in pairs.

Approach

▼ Discuss the three extracts with the whole group and some of the key changes which affected travel and sending messages.

TRANSPORT AND COMMUNICATIONS

The following sources.

Source A

'Everything is near, everything is immediate; time, distance and delay are abolished.'

Sydney Smith (writer and clergyman), 1842

Source B

'Does not the railway take the third class passenger at the same speed (as) royalty? Science has come down to the humblest of people and has given them advantages far greater than it gives the rich, because, although it has increased the power of the wealthy, it has given the poor a power which they did not at all possess.'

John Bright, Liberal M.P.

Source C

'A man may now cram into 10 years as much experience as his grandfather could have done in 50...The very streets bear evidence to the presence of the god of speed. What would Dr Johnson think if he strolled down Fleet Street today, with its network of telephone and telegraph wires above, that make it the very cradle of the world; with its endless stream of hansoms and buses and bicycles; with its future procession of motor cars?'

The Illustrated London News, 1897

Quotations A, B and C.

- What does each of them tell us about the attitudes and feelings of people at the time about these changes?
- How reliable and valuable is each extract for this purpose?

At the following information.

TRAVEL TIMES FROM LONDON

	1750	1830	1855
Brighton	1 day	5 hrs	3 hrs
Manchester	3 days	20 hrs	5 hrs
Edinburgh	10 days	45 hrs	13 hrs

This page may be photocopied for classroom use only

TRANSPORT AND COMMUNICATIONS

Developments in Communications

1837 First telegraph line set up between Euston and Camden in London.

1838 An American, Samuel Morse, invented a code using dots and dashes for each letter of the alphabet.

1840 Letters cost one penny to post. Railways made fast delivery possible.

1865 Telegraph cable laid across the Atlantic.

1870 Post Office took over the telegraph service, sending boys to deliver over 11 million messages.

1873 Cable from Britain to Australia; messages had previously taken 2 months.
First typewriters produced in America.

1876 Alexander Graham Bell, an American teacher, found a way of sending vocal messages along a wire using electric pulses. The invention was developed by Thomas Edison; soon wires spread across America and Europe.

1887 First electric underground trains in London.

1890 Electric trams introduced.

1896 The Italian inventor, Marconi, set up a company selling wireless sets to ships for sending Morse code messages.

1896 Cars permitted on British roads with a speed limit of 19 km per hour.

Developments in Printing

1785 *The Times* first appeared; by then 50 newspapers were being published in London.

1798 The first iron printing press, powered by a steam engine, was used.

1840s Fixed type around the outside of a roller could print 2 000 sheets an hour. When the paper was fed into the machine from a huge roll, over 24 000 sheets an hour were produced.

1855 Tax of a penny a sheet on newspapers was removed.

1896 *Daily Mail* appeared with articles about people rather than politics.

- Identify the progress in transport and communication achieved by 1850 and 1900.
- Write a paragraph for each of these years describing the way you could travel and send messages around Britain and beyond.
- In what part of everyday life was the impact of new inventions and developments most apparent?

- Draw up your own list of three major changes in transport and communication in the 20th century.
- Have they made as much difference to everyday life as those of the previous 100 years?

11. ANGLICANS AND METHODISTS

READ The following text.

In the 19th century Christian beliefs were challenged by new scientific discoveries. One of the most significant was the idea that Man had evolved over millions of years from much more primitive creatures such as monkeys.

From the amoeba to the 30 metres-long blue whale, and trees which weigh thousands of tonnes, all life is structured upon cells of a similar size. The theory that all living things evolved from one common source became generally accepted among naturalists during the 19th century.

In his book *The Origin of Species* (1859) Charles Darwin argued that the surviving species had been modified by natural selection. As his colleague, Alfred Wallace wrote, 'In every generation the inferior would inevitably be killed off... the fittest would survive.'

The idea shocked many Victorians who believed in the Biblical story of the creation of Man in the image of God. This bald and bearded biologist was claiming that the Book of Genesis, including the story of Adam and Eve, was fiction. The whole notion of a Divine Being creating life on Earth seemed to be threatened. Geologists had already raised doubts by asserting that rocks showed millions of years of change. Now Man was being shown as merely a superior form of animal.

Cartoonists had a field day, drawing gorillas in evening dress and Darwin as a monkey. The shy Darwin permitted his friend Thomas Huxley to defend his theory in a famous debate at Oxford in 1860. (See source A.) 'Darwin's bull dog', as Huxley liked to call himself, won a clear victory for Biology and Science over the Church.

These two strands - the scientific and the religious - have continued the debate over Darwin's theory since 1859. The sources provide a selection of these views. They show that our interpretations of the past - both historic and prehistoric - are themselves evolving. Both science and history are alive and changing as fresh minds investigate the evidence and assertions of their predecessors.

A typical cartoon making fun of Darwin's theories

ANGLICANS AND METHODISTS

READ The following sources and answer the questions below.

Source A

After speaking for half an hour, Wilberforce came to a point which linked the theory of evolution to a Victorian mother. 'Let me ask Mr Huxley just one question. Is it through his grandfather or his grandmother that he claims descent from a monkey?'

Mr Huxley slowly and deliberately arose... very quiet and very grave he spoke, 'An ape may seem to you to be a poor sort of creature, of low intelligence and stooping gait... But I would rather have an ape for an ancestor than a man who is prepared to use his great gifts to obscure the truth.'

The Oxford Debate between Bishop Samuel Wilberforce and Thomas Huxley

Source B

'I have no patience whatever with these gorilla damnifications of humanity.'

Thomas Carlyle (1795-1881)

Source C

'The impact of *The Origin of Species* lay in the simplicity of its main idea: evolution meant natural selection. "The weak go to the wall and the strong succeed," reflected a fact of life in capitalist society.'

Modern historian

Source D

'The Big Lie - Exposed! God made it so that animals cannot change into other animals. A dog will always be a dog, never ever a cat. And, of course, a monkey can never change into a man. When people believe in evolution they don't believe in God. They think they come from animals so they act like animals! They think God can't see them. Boy, are they going to be surprised when they die and find out God is real!'

Caption from a Creationist comic strip

Source E

In 1972 the State Board of Education in California approved equal treatment in textbooks for the teaching of both evolution and the doctrine of Creation as described in the Bible. In 1979 a Gallup poll found that half of American adults 'believe God created Adam and Eve to start the human race'.

Creation versus Evolution today

- Write two paragraphs.
  - ▼ One which gives a view of Darwin and the Oxford debate from the point of view of a Christian who believes in the literal truth of the Bible.
  - ▼ One which gives the view of a Christian who accepts the idea of evolution.
- Compare your ideas with a friend and sum up the key points for a wall display showing the differing interpretations of the controversy over Darwin's book.
- How has the controversy changed since 1859?
- What are your views on the main issues involved?

12. THE EFFECTS OF THE FRENCH WARS

READ   The following text.

The French Revolution of 1789 was followed by the banning of trade unions which appeared to threaten the established order in society. However, the most violent demonstrations of unrest among workers during the French Wars resulted from economic distress.

Textile workers, claiming to follow a mysterious leader, Ned Ludd, smashed machines and set fire to mills in the north of England. They were not only protesting against machines in mills instead of looms based in the weaver's cottage. Most were mill workers who saw all further changes as a threat to their livelihood. They also disliked working long hours and being paid in tokens which could only be spent at the factory owners' shops.

An artist's impression of Ned Ludd

Events

1811   Wide frames had been introduced into Nottingham lace mills. Wage cuts and redundancies followed.

March 11th, 60 wide frames were destroyed. The unrest lasted a year and by December about 1000 frames had been smashed.

1812   In January mill burning began in the West Riding of Yorkshire. Wool workers, called 'croppers', found their task of trimming the rough threads of the textile threatened by new shearing machines.

April 11th, 150 workers marched on William Cartwright's mill near Huddersfield. Two Luddites were shot by troops guarding the property. Cartwright would not allow them to receive medical treatment until they gave the names of their accomplices. Both men died. A week later Cartwright narrowly avoided a murder attempt but another mill owner, William Horsfall, was shot. Three Luddites were found guilty and hanged. Fourteen more were executed for their attack on the mill.

Meanwhile in Lancashire 11 Luddites were killed during an attack on a power loom factory at Middleton. Twelve more were tried and hanged.

1816   Apart from one more riot at Loughborough in 1816, the unrest ended and trade conditions improved.

THE EFFECTS OF THE FRENCH WARS

READ The following sources and answer the questions below.

Source A

'Sir,
Information has just been given that you are a holder of those DETESTABLE SHEARING MACHINES. You will take notice that if they are not taken down by the end of next week I shall attach one of my Lieutenants to destroy them... and if you have the impudence to fire at any of my men they have orders to murder you and burn all your housing.

Ned Ludd'
A Luddite Letter to Mr Smith of Huddersfield

Source B

'The attack on Daniel Burton's power loom mill in Middleton was made by a crowd of several thousands ... At the head of these armed bandits a Man of Straw was carried, representing the renowned General Ludd whose standard-bearer waved a sort of red flag.'
The 'Leeds Mercury', April 1812

Source C

'Luddites have in view ultimately to overturn the system of government by revolutionising the country.'
Evidence from a government informer at Barnsley, 1812

Source D

'... nothing but absolute want could have driven a large, and once honest and industrious body of the people, into the commission of excesses so hazardous... You call these men a mob ... Are we aware of our obligations to a mob? It is the mob that labour in our fields and serve in our houses, that man our navy, and recruit our army, that have enabled us to defy all the world, and can also defy us when neglect and calamity have driven them to despair... Is there not blood enough upon our penal code, that more must be poured forth to ascend to Heaven and testify against us?... Are these the remedies for a starving and desperate populace?'
Lord Byron speaking in the House of Lords on the Bill to make machine breaking punishable by death, 27 February 1812

Source E

'Despite the government's fear that Luddism might herald a political revolution like France in 1789, there is little evidence to suggest that these skilled workers were interested in such ideas. Nor did the Luddites see themselves as part of a 'working class' which had common grievances against employers. Each group had particular concerns which grew into violent protest out of anger and fear of unemployment. News of riots elsewhere certainly did nothing to discourage such feelings but there was no conspiracy between the Luddites in each area.'
A modern historian's view

- What evidence in sources A and B might have encouraged a connection between Luddism and the French Revolution?
- What appear to have been the major causes of unrest?
- What differences can you find between the affected areas?
- Sum up the main points made by Lord Byron in source D.
- If source E is correct, what does it tell us about the attitude of the government and its informers?
- Would you say that Luddism was an effect of the French Wars or not?
- Try to find one argument for and one against.

13. CORN LAWS AND FREE TRADE

Aim

To show an awareness of different ideas and attitudes and how different causes of an event are connected.

Introduction

This unit develops the viewpoints and interpretations which are introduced in the Core Text.

Resources

Photocopiable sheet page 28 and Core Text Unit 16.

Objective: for pupils to take part in a debate in order to understand the arguments for and against the repeal of the Corn Laws in 1846.

Skills: analysis; preparing and presenting an argument.

Organisation

Divide the teaching group in half. The chairs can be arranged so that each group is facing the other with one member seated in front of the rest. This pupil will be the spokesperson for or against repeal.

Approach

▼ Members of each group use the Core Text and their notes to jot down at least two points to support their case.

▼ The resource sheets, divided in half, are distributed to the appropriate half of the class so that these additional points can also be used in the discussion.

▼ Only the spokesperson can speak in the discussion. This opens formally with a statement by the spokesperson giving one main reason why she/he supports or opposes the Corn Laws.

▼ Each spokesperson then takes it in turn to express another point from members of the group who whisper to her/him so that the other side cannot hear.

▼ The discussion will develop a momentum of its own as each side tries to answer the points made. It is important that this is allowed to happen so that both facts and opinions can be expressed along with some of the passion felt by participants.

▼ It is concluded after an agreed period of time by the teacher. The exercise can be reviewed through a whole group discussion. The points made can be used to reinforce understanding of the topic by asking all pupils to note down three additional points for or against the Corn Laws which emerged from the discussion.

CORN LAWS AND FREE TRADE

Facts And Opinions In Favour Of The Corn Laws

Factory owners want repeal so they can pay lower wages.

The Corn Laws are needed to protect British farmers.

Farmers deserve good prices for the food they grow; they have invested in new farming methods and equipment.

The Poor Rate is crippling farmers; they need decent returns for their crops in order to pay it.

Landowners are the backbone of British society. Not to protect them from foreign farmers would be madness.

If landowners cannot have good prices for their produce they will have to get rid of farm labourers.

If workers in towns are hungry then their employers are to blame for paying them so little, not the farmers!

The abolitionists are revolutionaries in disguise; they want to overthrow the men of property in England.

Facts And Opinions In Favour Of Repealing The Corn Laws

Working people are going hungry, including farm workers, to preserve the profits of the big landowners.

The Irish are starving. We cannot send them surplus bread because the Corn Laws make sure this is not grown.

Free Trade is the solution to our economic problems, not protection. Allow foreigners to sell us their food and they will be able to buy our manufactured goods.

Free and fair competition in all products will bring an era of peace and plenty. Protection means scarcity, jealousy and greed; it causes wars.

Free Trade will mean cheap food and increased employment as all industries prosper.

The Corn Laws encourage too much wheat production rather than mixed dairy and arable farming.

The home market will not be flooded with cheap foreign food; transport costs will prevent that.

The Corn Laws harm the poor mainly; they add 20% to a weaver's food bill but less than 1% to a nobleman's.

14. RADIO MANCHESTER 1819

It is Monday 16th August, 1819. The campaign for parliamentary reform giving more seats to factory towns and the vote to every adult male has been underway for several years. The leading national figure is Henry Hunt, a tall proud man with a voice as clear as a bell. He is coming to address a meeting at St Peter's Fields in central Manchester. Long processions of working people, carrying banners demanding 'Universal Suffrage','Vote by Ballot' and 'Annual Parliaments', are converging on the area. Local magistrates have expressed fears of a deliberate riot and have sought permission from the government to call out the Manchester Yeomanry Cavalry to stand by. Regular troops - the 11th Hussars - have also been sent to the city.

- Form small groups of three or four. Your radio team has been asked to prepare news reports at 8 a.m. and 8 p.m. on Monday 16th August 1819.

The sources of information for the two broadcasts.
- Try to report the facts even though most of your sources will show some kind of bias.
- You can interview some eye witnesses.
- Begin with background details to help set the scene for that warm and sunny morning.
- If you can, use a word processor to arrange your script.

Information for the 8 a.m. Programme

Source A

'Urged on by the harangues of a few desperate demagogues, we anticipate at no distant period a general rising...'
Five Lancashire magistrates writing to the Home Secretary, July 1st 1819

Source B

'...even if they (the radicals) should utter sedition...it will be the wisest course to abstain from any endeavour to disperse the mob, unless they should proceed to acts of felony or riot.'
A letter from the Home Office to magistrates in Manchester, August 4th 1819

Source C

'...all the accounts tend to show that the worst possible spirit pervades the country... I hope peace may be preserved, but under all circumstances it is scarcely possible to expect it.'
Mr Norris, a local magistrate, writing to the Home Office, August 15th 1819

Source D

In July reports reached the magistrates that some of the workers had been drilling and would be armed. To keep order they had 400 special constables, 600 Hussars (army cavalry) and at least 400 mounted Yeomanry (local volunteers) ready to deal with any problems.

This page may be photocopied for classroom use only

RADIO MANCHESTER 1819

Information for the 8 p.m. Programme

Source E

A summary of the day's events

11 a.m. The magistrates met and eventually agreed that Hunt should be arrested at 1 p.m. Henry Hunt arrived at the meeting, estimated at 60 000 which was nearly half the population of south-east Lancashire. Over 1 500 constables, volunteer and regular soldiers were present.

1.40 p.m. Hunt was arrested as he began to speak. There was panic and a small pocket of resistance to the Yeomanry with some shots being fired.

2 p.m. The field was cleared; 11 people had died and over 400 were injured.

Source F

'...the Manchester Yeomanry Cavalry rode into the mob, which gave way before them...all was quiet and orderly...As soon as Hunt and Johnson had jumped from the waggon, a cry was made by the cavalry, 'Get their flags'. In consequence, they immediately dashed not only at the flags which were in the waggon, but at those which were posted among the crowd, cutting most indiscriminately...in order to get at them. This set the people running in all directions, and it was not till this act had been committed that any brick-bats were hurled at the military. From that moment the Manchester Yeomanry Cavalry lost all command of temper.'

John Tyas, reporter for The Times

Source G

'...their sabres were plied to hew a way through naked held-up hands and defenceless heads; and then chopped limbs and wound-gaping skulls were seen; and cries and groans were mingled with the din of that horrid confusion...In ten minutes...the field was an almost deserted space...The Yeomanry had dismounted...some were wiping their sabres. Several mounds of human beings were where they had fallen, crushed down.'

Samuel Bamford, a Radical eye witness

Source H

'I was never in such danger at Waterloo for at Waterloo it was man to man but at Manchester it was downright murder.'

John Lees, eye witness and ex-soldier

Mr Lees was badly injured; he had a sabre gash on his shoulder and a deep cut on his arm. He was severely bruised when a Cavalry horse was ridden over him.

Source I

'The large crowd estimated at about 60 000 people had gathered illegally in the field near to St Peter's Church. As Henry Hunt and other noted Radical leaders arrived it became evident that there was a danger of insurrection and riot.'

Statement by William Hulton, Chairman of the Manchester Magistrates

Source J

'...the Manchester troop of Yeomanry...were scattered singly or in small groups over the greater part of the Field, literally hemmed up and hedged into the mob so that they were powerless either to make an impression or to escape; in fact, they were in the power of those whom they were designed to overawe, and it required only a glance to discover their helpless position, and the necessity of our being brought to their rescue.'

A statement by Lieutenant Joliffe of the Hussars

Source K

'The Cavalry struck at no one en route to the hustings, not a sabre was used until they were assailed by the mob, the avenues of escape were never blocked. As Yeomanry Cavalry they did not feel it necessary to defend their conduct, for they had done no wrong.'

Statement by the Manchester Yeomanry Cavalry

Source L

'The whole town of Manchester was grateful for the magistrates' firm, prompt and decisive action.'

Reverend Hay, a local magistrate

Sketch plan of St Peter's Fields

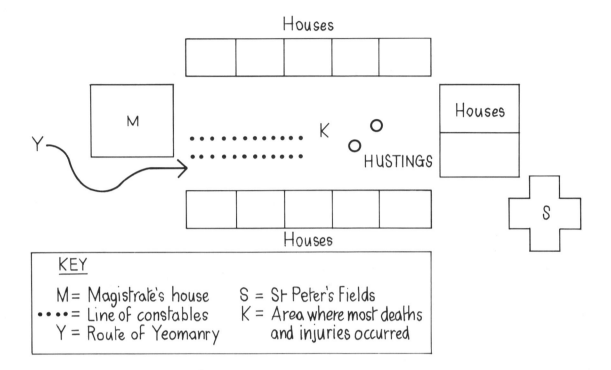

KEY

M = Magistrate's house   S = St Peter's Fields
•••• = Line of constables   K = Area where most deaths
Y = Route of Yeomanry   and injuries occurred

- Look carefully at the above plan.
- Sketch in the crowd of people listening to Hunt.
- Explain why panic may have set in, and why so many deaths and injuries may have occurred.
  CLUE TO SUCCESS: Think about how many exits there were for the crowds. How accessible were they to people in the middle of the crowd?

At the modern view in source M.

Source M

'When the unarmed marchers arrived that day at St Peter's Fields determined to protest peacefully, the cavalry with chilling brutality bugle-charged and maniacally hacked with their sabres...I wish I could feel...confident that it will never happen again.'

Robert Clark, The Guardian, *1 August 1989*

- How far do you agree with this summary of the incident?
- Write a brief comment giving a different interpretation.
- What groups in society today might support each view?

15. THE GROWTH OF TRADE UNIONS

READ The following text and look carefully at the cartoons.

After the failure of Robert Owen's 'Grand National' union the victims of unemployment gave more support to the political movement of Chartism than to trade unions. The unions survived mainly among craftsmen who wanted to protect their livelihood by regulating the number of entrants into their trade.

Between 1850 and 1875 the 'New Model Unions' were successful. They represented skilled workers such as carpenters, joiners, ironfounders and millwrights. The Amalgamated Society of Engineers had a high subscription of 1s. (5p) a week and a full time General Secretary based at its London headquarters. It provided sickness, pension and funeral benefits. Unions could operate legally as friendly societies. They lobbied MPs for more rights, had direct contact with their network of branches and large strike funds.

Other workers could not afford to set up such national unions but locally they had influence on Committees called Trades Councils. In 1868 the Manchester Trades Council took the lead in calling a Trades Union Congress to discuss common problems. The TUC soon became an important pressure group campaigning for legal protection of trade unions. In 1871 the Liberal Government passed an Act giving unions the right to exist and protecting their funds. In 1875 the Conservative Government supported laws allowing peaceful picketing and preventing employers having striking workers arrested.

Economic depression in the later 1870s brought high unemployment and a decline in trade union membership. At the end of the 1880s the economy improved; a series of successful strikes by girls in Bryant and May's East End match factory in 1888 and London dockers in 1889 led to the formation of large new unions of mainly unskilled workers. Socialists like Tom Mann and Ben Tillett saw them as the starting point for creating societies in which state control brought a greater distribution of wealth to the worker.

In the 1890s the employers counterattacked, employing non-union workers in the docks, gas and engineering industries. Finally in 1900 the Taff Vale Railway Company in South Wales sued a union for its loss of income during a strike. The same year saw the birth of the Labour Party supported by trade unions which were still fighting to protect their right to strike.

1800-35: Trade Unions suppressed by Government and employers

1850-75: New Model Unions, respectable skilled workers

THE GROWTH OF TRADE UNIONS

1880s: *Growth of the New Unions for the unskilled*

1890s: *Employers counterattack: Labour Party formed*

The text and cartoons show two kinds of interpretation of the growth of trade unions.
- The four cartoons suggest there were four clear stages in their growth. How accurate is this according to the text?
- What are the strengths and weaknesses of cartoons compared with a written account as a way of understanding history?

The views of some modern historians in the sources below.
- In your own words, sum up the main point made in each extract. Try to separate the facts from the opinions.
- Which one is most biased in favour of trade unions?
- Does this make it the least useful in helping you to understand the topic?

Source A

In the 1820s the trade unionists did not realise that higher wages meant lower profits. If investors could not obtain good interest rates from industry, they would put their money elsewhere and the workers would suffer. The trade unions were basically conservative, trying to resist new machinery and looking back to a time when a weaver's loom was in his cottage.

Source B

The leaders of the New Model Unions shared the attitudes and values of their employers. They dressed, behaved and, after 1867, voted like their masters. Both wanted to protect their livelihood against those who wanted fairer shares of jobs and wealth and state control, instead of private ownership.

Source C

In the 1880s, Britain trailed behind America and Germany in her industry, and the term 'unemployed' was used for the first time. The unions blindly fought to save jobs and opposed the introduction of new machinery. They were as conservative as their masters. Even as late as 1900 there were only two million trade union members out of a total national labour force of over 16 million.

Source D

Factory owners, and the upper classes who looked down on them, wanted to give the impression that trade union leaders were revolutionaries trying to overturn the social order by starting strikes and destroying lives and property. So laws were passed against unions. The Church told the poor to be satisfied with their lot and they would be rewarded in heaven.

16. THE GREAT EXHIBITION OF 1851

Aim

To consider the causes and significance of the event.

Introduction

The most significant British event between the Great Reform Acts of 1832 and 1867 was probably the Great Exhibition. Nowadays such events are commonplace. Annual exhibitions provide shop windows for new cars, boats, clothes, toys, homes - anything you can think of. Garden Festivals, Theme Parks and World Fairs or Expos attract millions of visitors anxious to laugh, learn and, of course, buy! London's Hyde Park was the site for the first such international exhibition.

Resources

Photocopiable pupil sheet page 35.

Objective: to examine the different types of cause and consequence.
Skill: analysis and comparison of sources; group discussion.

Organisation

Pupils should work individually, and then in pairs for the final activity.

Approach

▼ Introduce the topic using the resource sheet and any other relevant illustrations e.g. books on the Crystal Palace or mid-Victorian England.
▼ Discussion on the broad task of interpreting the causes and the outcome. The latter requires pupils to offer their own ideas in the light of such events today.

THE GREAT EXHIBITION OF 1851

READ Sources A to F and answer the questions below.

Source A

The full title, The Great Exhibition of the Works of Industry of All Nations, indicates that the intention was to show how large a lead the Industrial Revolution had given Britain over her rivals. The new factories supplied a world market. With a strong navy, a global empire and a popular young queen, Britain was confident and secure with much to celebrate and show off.

Britain in 1851, *A modern historian's view*

Source B

Prince Albert was the main organiser. Henry Cole, an industrial designer, knew how to keep officials on their toes. Joseph Paxton, a former head gardener at Chatsworth House, designed the Crystal Palace. It was no coincidence that it looked like a mammoth greenhouse. The structure of a lily leaf inspired the design of the roof. Expenses were met by a public subscription, launched 15 months before the opening.

Adapted from Eric de Mare, London 1851

Source C

'This is one of the greatest and most glorious days of our lives, with which, to my pride and joy, the name of my dearly beloved Albert is for ever associated!'

The Queen's delight at the opening

Among 100 000 objects, including works of art, one major aspect intrigued Victoria, 'What used to be done by hand and used to take months doing is now accomplished in a few instants by the most beautiful machinery.'

Source D

The whole world seemed to be coming to the Great Exhibition. In its 140 days 6 201 856 people came from home and abroad. London's bus companies, hotels and boarding houses all made good profits. At its height over 90 000 people filled the exhibition. After three weeks the entrance fee fell from 25p to 5p from Mondays to Thursdays. No alcohol, smoking or dogs were permitted. Sometimes whole parishes came, led by their vicar.

According to the Catalogue, 'in the Central Area are sold ices (kept frozen by steam), pastry, sandwiches, patties, fruits, tea, coffee, cocoa, lemonade, seltzer and soda water.' The caterers, Schweppes, made a profit of £45 000. Paxton's Palace was re-built in a large park in south London. In 1936 it burnt down.

A modern historian's view

Source E

'This will long be remembered as a singularly happy year of peace, plenty, good feeling, innocent pleasure, national glory of the best and purest sort.' 1851 and All That, *Lord Macaulay, Victorian writer*

- Why did the Exhibition happen there and then?
- How was the Exhibition organised and built?
- What made it so successful?
- Compare the main features of the Great Exhibition with similar events today.
- With a partner, draw up a list of the main differences and give reasons for these.

17. POLITICAL REFORM FOR WOMEN

Units 19 and 20 in the Core Text. You will remember that the Act of 1867 gave the vote to all men over 21 who lived in towns. Men who lived in the countryside had to wait until 1884 before they were given the vote. Notice that these Acts only refer to men, even though women stood alongside their husbands, fathers and brothers at meetings and demonstrations. However, women were not given the vote until 1918 and then they had to be over 30. It was 1928 before women could vote at the same age as men, at 21.

- Look carefully at the list of events below, which show the process leading to women being given the vote.
- Draw a line to the scale 2cm = 10 years. You should begin with the year 1840 and end with 1930.
- Place the events below in chronological order on your time line.

1870 Women allowed to serve on the new School Boards.

1869 Women given the right to vote in municipal elections.

1861 John Stuart Mill wrote *Considerations on Representative Government*, in which he argued both men and women should be given the vote.

1886 Act passed which allowed a deserted wife to sue her husband for maintenance.

1851 Anne Knight, a Quaker, actively campaigned for universal suffrage for men and women.

1840 R. J. Richardson, a leading male radical, wrote a pamphlet called *The Rights of Women* which supported women's right to vote.

1867 Reform Act excluded women.

1870 First separate Women's Suffrage Bill defeated in Parliament.

1913 Emily Davison, a suffragette, killed when she threw herself under the King's horse at the Derby.

1913 Cat and Mouse Act allowed suffragettes on hunger strike in prison to be released and then re-arrested when stronger.

1868 Lydia Becker founded the Women's Suffrage Journal.

1897 National Union of Women's Suffrage Societies founded.

1914 Outbreak of First World War. Women's movement supported Britain and as a result the status of women improved.

1905 First Suffragettes imprisoned for violent behaviour.

1884 Third Reform Act. Women still not given the vote.

1918 Representation of the People Act gave votes to women over 30.

1889 *An Appeal Against Female Suffrage* published.

1912 Emmeline Pankhurst imprisoned.

1928 Equal Franchise Act gave votes to women aged 21.

1903 Emmeline Pankhurst founded the Women's Social and Political Union.

POLITICAL REFORM FOR WOMEN

All the sources on these two pages.

- Cut up the sheets into separate sources.
- Sort the sources into the following groups:
  - ▼ Sources written by men who supported the idea that women should have the vote.
  - ▼ Sources written by men who did not support women's suffrage.
  - ▼ Sources written by women who wanted the vote.
  - ▼ Sources written by women who did not support the idea of women's suffrage.
- For each group of sources:
  - ▼ Explain the attitudes and ideas of those who wrote them.
  - ▼ Explain why you think they held such attitudes and ideas. Consider the background of the writers; whether they were rich or poor; the traditions of the time.

Source A

'I take early opportunity of writing to beg those patriotic women as members of the National Charter Association to aid their brethren...It will now dishonour (men) to go on repeating their demand for only men when it is so widely spread and acknowledged that every adult member of the human family...has the same right to vote.'

Anne Knight, 1851

Source B

'Ought women to interfere in the political affairs of the country?...I do most distinctly...say - Yes!...she has a natural right...a political right...a civil right...It is nowhere written in the...civil law that woman by reason of her sex, is disqualified from the exercise of political right.'

The Rights of Women, *Mr R.J. Richardson, 1840*

Source C

'In the preceding argument for universal, but graduated suffrage, I have taken no account of difference of sex. All human beings have the same interest in good government... and they have equal need of a voice in it to secure their share of its benefits.'

Considerations on Representative Government, *John Stuart Mill, 1861*

Source D

'The Queen is most anxious to enlist everyone who can speak or write to join in checking this mad, wicked folly of "Women's Rights"...on which her poor feeble sex is bent, forgetting every sense of womanly feeling and propriety.'

Written by Queen Victoria, c. 1870s

POLITICAL REFORM FOR WOMEN

Source E

'That women as a body desire a vote in Parliament I do not think. The women who do have such a wish form but a very small proportion of those whose opinions they say they represent.'

The Englishwoman's Domestic Magazine, 1870

Source F

'(We) strongly protest against the proposed parliamentary franchise to women...(It is) distasteful to the great majority of women and mischievous both to themselves and the state.'

A manifesto published in 1889 by women who later formed the Women's National Anti-suffrage League

Source G

'Women claim votes, not because they are, or want to be LIKE MEN but because they are different and have somewhat different views. They want the vote as a tool, with which to do not Men's Work, but Women's Work, which men have left undone or are trying unsuccessfully to do.'

Handbill distributed by the National Union of Women's Suffrage Societies

Source H

'The failure to recognise that man is the master...lies at the root of the suffrage movement...By leaving out of account those powers of the mind in which man is the superior, woman falls into the error of thinking that she can really compete with him.'

The Unexpurgated Case Against Woman Suffrage *by Sir Almoth Wright, 1913*

Source I

'Put me upon an island where the girls are few, Put me among the most ferocious lions in the zoo, You can put me on a treadmill, and I'll never, never fret, But for pity's sake, don't put me near a suffragette!'

A musical song of the early 1890s

Source J

'I cannot wonder that people of excitable temperament have been goaded almost to madness by the "shuffling and delay" with which our question has been treated in Parliament. If men had been treated by the House of Commons as women have been treated there would have been bloody reprisals all over the country...what is called militancy is "political unrest" caused by mishandling and misunderstanding by politicians of one of the greatest movements (women's movements) in the history of the world.'

Millicent Fawcett c.1908

18. FACTORY AND MINE REFORM

In this activity you are going to use historical evidence to decide whether statements are true or false.

At Unit 21 in the Core Text.
- Either work alone, or with a partner.
- In your exercise book write out the title:
  'Factory and Mine Reform: True or False Game'.
- Write out the first statement from below.
- Using the source material in Unit 21 decide whether the statement is true or false, and write your answer beside the statement.
- Now write out a short quotation from the source material to prove that your answer is correct.
- The first statement is completed for you as an example.

Statements

1. When Robert Owen's cotton supplies did not arrive he paid half wages to his employees. FALSE.

   Supporting evidence: 'When cotton supplies failed for four months I paid full wages for only keeping the machinery clean and in good working condition.' From a book written by Robert Owen.

2. In 1816 Robert Peel was Prime Minister.

3. A committee investigating children's working conditions had Richard Oastler as Chairman.

4. Peel's 1802 Factory Act allowed pauper children to work for only 16 hours a day.

5. In 1819 children under 9 years could work in cotton mills.

6. After 1842 women were not allowed to work underground.

7. Men and women had to work no longer than 10 hours a day after 1847.

8. No children under the age of 10 years were allowed to work at all once the Act of 1878 had been passed.

Source H in Unit 21.

- Describe what is happening.
- How do you think the children felt?
- Using Unit 21, explain how your life today is different to that of a working child during the 1840s.

19. CHOLERA AND PUBLIC HEALTH

When people came to live in the new industrial towns during the 1800s, houses had to be built very quickly. They were built without toilets or sewage systems, so most families had to share earth closets. In one part of a factory town there were only 33 lavatories for 7000 people.

Earth Closets

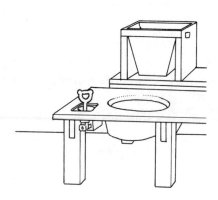

Moule's Earth Closet of 1860

In Moule's Earth Closet, the human waste fell into the closet and then the handle on the left was pulled to release ash or earth from the hopper above the seat. This fell onto the human waste. These earth closets were built in rows outside people's houses. They were supposed to be emptied every week by 'night soil' workers. However, many were hardly ever emptied. As a result they gave off a foul smell. Many of these closets simply drained into cesspits or rivers. The river water was then used for drinking and so the water supply became contaminated and disease spread very quickly.

At the picture of the earth closet, and read the text carefully.
- Label the operating handle and the ash hopper.
- What were the disadvantages of this lavatory?
- Why do you think people of the time were prepared to put up with foul smelling toilets which had to be shared with many others?

Water Closets

Several people had worked on ideas for water closets. For example, Sir John Harington invented the first water closet in 1596. However, not many people took it seriously, because it needed a supply of running water and very few towns had this. In 1778 Bramah designed a closet with two valves. One let water into the bowl and the other let the water drain out. During the 1800s thousands of these were sold to wealthy people.

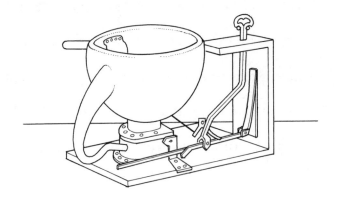

Bramah's Closet, 1778

At the diagram of Bramah's Water Closet and read the text carefully.
- Explain how you think Bramah's closet worked. It might help if you label parts of the diagram.
- Why do you think only wealthy people bought Bramah's closet?

CHOLERA AND PUBLIC HEALTH

Bostel's Wash Down Closet

In 1889 an Englishman called Bostel invented a wash down closet similar to the one we use today. It was made by Doultons. The closet was very noisy and often so badly installed that it was a greater health risk than the outside earth closets.

Bostel's Wash Down Closet ▶

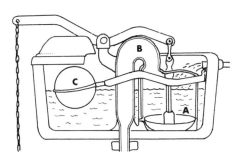

◀ *The cistern*
When the chain was pulled A rose up and forced water over the bend marked B. This emptied the cistern into the toilet bowl. The cistern then refilled. C floated to the top and cut off the water once the cistern was full.

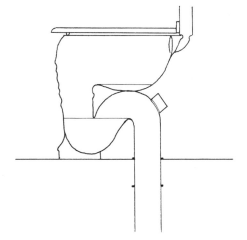

A cross-section of the wash down closet ▶
Notice that a small amount of water was left in the bowl to act as a seal.

LOOK

At the above diagrams and read the text carefully.
- What other supplies or developments were needed in and around people's houses for water closets to work successfully?
- Why do you think people were slow to install water closets?
- What effects might the introduction of water closets have had on people's health?
- Using writing and drawings make a chart showing the chronological development of toilets.

20. MEDICINE

READ The following text carefully and answer the questions below.

From early times women were expected to have a knowledge of how to cure everyday illnesses. However, even in the 1800s women were not allowed to train as doctors. During the 19th century several women tried to bring about a change in attitude towards women in medicine. One of these women was Elizabeth Garrett Anderson, who became the first woman to qualify as a doctor in Britain.

Born into a wealthy family in 1836, Elizabeth was fortunate in having a father who believed that his daughters should be educated. When she was 24 she met one of the first women doctors, Elizabeth Blackwell, who was on a visit to England from America. This made Elizabeth Garrett Anderson decide that she too would become a doctor.

Although her father was against this, Elizabeth eventually won him round. At first she worked as a nurse, then she began attending medical lectures. However, the male students complained. They said that her presence in the operating theatre was '...an outrage on our natural instincts and feelings...' and that it would destroy the respect which men had for women. So Elizabeth persuaded some medical professors to give her private lessons and she passed all her examinations.

Now Elizabeth had to be accepted by one of the three leading medical societies. The College of Physicians and the College of Surgeons had rules against accepting women, so Elizabeth applied to the third, the Society of Apothecaries. However, they refused to accept her as she was a woman, so Elizabeth's father took them to court and forced them to accept her. After this the Society changed its rules to stop other women getting in.

Elizabeth was now able to work as a doctor but as no British university would accept her, it took another five years for her to become a full doctor of medicine. In the end she completed her studies in Paris.

Elizabeth's first post was at St Mary's Dispensary in London where medical help was available to poor women. Eventually the hospital was completely staffed with female doctors and became known as the New Hospital for Women. In 1871 Elizabeth married but she continued with her work and helped other women to become educated and accepted by the medical profession.

- How much do you think that Elizabeth's family background and her wealthy father helped her to become a doctor?
- Why do you think that men were so against women entering the medical profession?
- Do you think Elizabeth was typical of women born in the 1830s? Give reasons for your answer.
- To what extent do you think that Elizabeth encouraged other women to enter the medical profession?

21. EDUCATION

Aim To organise a dramatic reconstruction of the monitorial system of education.

Resources Photocopiable pupil resource sheets pages 44 and 45.

Organisation
- ▼ Provide pupils with the instruction sheet giving details about the dramatic reconstruction.
- ▼ It is suggested that the teacher should play the role of the TEACHER in charge of the monitor school.
- ▼ After pupils have researched the monitorial system give one envelope to each group with sufficient role cards for one per pupil. Each envelope should have only one MONITOR card.
- ▼ Once each group has established their roles call the monitors to you and give one LESSON INSTRUCTION sheet to each monitor. If there are more than four groups the lesson instructions can be duplicated.
- ▼ The MONITORS should now teach their group using rote learning.
- ▼ Allow about 15 minutes for this activity. Then stop all groups.
- ▼ You should now test each group to establish how much they have learnt.
- ▼ Children who learnt their lessons were awarded MERIT BADGES. When a certain number of merit badges had been received they could be exchanged for bats, balls or kites. Those who did not learn their lessons had to wear a wooden log around their neck, shackles on their legs or they were suspended from the ceiling in a basket. Children who came to school with dirty faces had to have them washed in front of the whole school.

Follow-up *This could centre around discussion based on the questions in the activities section. Pupils could also discuss why the lessons were often religious. It is interesting for both pupils and monitors to explain how they felt during the dramatic reconstruction.*

Role cards

MONITOR
- You are directly responsible to your teacher who is in charge of the school.
- You must obey your teacher and carry out the instructions you are given.
- You are expected to teach the pupils in your group the information which your teacher will give you.
- Teach the information using rote learning.
- You expect the pupils to obey you.

PUPILS
- You are very poor and underfed.
- You have fleas which make you itch and sores on your skin.
- You have very poor eyesight but no glasses.
- You may have an illness, but not bad enough to be away from school.
- You are expected to obey the teacher and the monitor INSTANTLY.

EDUCATION

Pupil Instruction Sheet.

- You are about to begin a dramatic reconstruction designed to help you learn more about education in the 1800s. Follow the instructions below carefully.

  ▼ Divide into groups of six or seven.
  ▼ Using any books available find out about the monitor system of education.
  CLUE TO SUCCESS: The names Joseph Lancaster (1801) and Andrew Bell (1797) might help you.
  ▼ When you think that you understand the monitor system, ask your teacher to come and listen to your group's explanation.
  ▼ Your teacher will give you an envelope which contains role cards. Place these face down on the table and select a card. Each person should now have a role card to follow.
  ▼ Read your role card carefully.
  ▼ The person with the MONITOR role card should ask your teacher for the lesson instructions.
  ▼ MONITORS should read these carefully and then teach the lesson to the other members of the group who will be pupils.
  ▼ The lesson should be taught using ROTE LEARNING. This means that the monitor will speak the lines to be learnt and the PUPILS will then repeat them, until they have learnt them off by heart.
  ▼ After a certain amount of time your teacher will come and inspect your group to see if they have learnt the information.

- Write up a diary of your experiences in the monitor school. Write your diary from the point of view of the character you played.
- What are the main differences between the monitor system and the way in which you are educated today?
- Why do you think that the monitor system was used in the early 1800s?

Using Unit 24 in the Core Text, make a list of the different types of schools which existed in the 19th century.

- Write a short paragraph describing each school.
- Which type of school would you most like to have attended? Explain your answer carefully.
- Can you think of any reasons why parents of poorer families may not have wanted their children to go to school?
- Identify any similarities between your education today and the education of young people in the 1800s.

Lesson Instructions

1. The Ten Commandments.

> You shall have no other gods before me.
> You shall not make yourself any idol.
> You shall not take the name of the Lord thy God in vain.
> Remember the sabbath day, and keep it holy.
> Honour your father and mother.
> You shall not kill.
> You shall not commit adultery.
> You shall not steal.
> You shall not bear false witness.
> You shall not covet.

2. Using an atlas teach your pupils the names of the major cities of the world. Your pupils should know which country each city is in.

3. The Creed.

> I believe in God the Father Almighty, maker of heaven and earth;
> and in Jesus Christ his only Son our Lord,
> who was conceived of the Holy Ghost,
> born of the Virgin Mary,
> suffered under Pontius Pilate,
> was crucified and buried,
> he descended into hell;
> on the third day he rose again from the dead,
> he ascended into heaven,
> and sitteth on the right hand of God the Father Almighty,
> from thence he shall come
> to judge the quick and the dead.

4. Teach your pupils the following tables:

1 x 3 = 3	1 x 7 = 7
2 x 3 = 6	2 x 7 = 14
3 x 3 = 9	3 x 7 = 21
4 x 3 = 12	4 x 7 = 28
5 x 3 = 15	5 x 7 = 35
6 x 3 = 18	6 x 7 = 42
7 x 3 = 21	7 x 7 = 49
8 x 3 = 24	8 x 7 = 56
9 x 3 = 27	9 x 7 = 63
10 x 3 = 30	10 x 7 = 70
11 x 3 = 33	11 x 7 = 77
12 x 3 = 36	12 x 7 = 84

22. HEART OF THE EMPIRE

READ The following text and sources A to F. Then answer the questions below.

For most of the 19th century the head of the British Empire was Queen Victoria. As Queen, Empress and mother she seemed to be the symbol of its unity, strength and permanence. On her Golden Jubilee in 1887 she was pictured with 55 members of her family, ten of whom became the monarchs of European states. Her Diamond Jubilee in 1897 was a celebration of her Empire, over 10 million square miles and nearly 400 million people. Amid all the colour and pageantry sat 'a little plain flushed old lady...all in black...so very quiet, so very grave...but also very glorious' wrote the *Daily Mail* reporter.

The title 'Great Mother', by which her American Indian subjects in Canada knew her, was highly appropriate. She and Prince Albert had had nine children in 21 years of marriage before his death in 1861. The family was the bedrock of Victorian society. Its pattern of a dominant father, the breadwinner whose word had to be obeyed, and a mother devoted to her children and the home was apparent throughout society. There was a strict hierarchy in which children and servants knew their place and behaved accordingly.

Of course domestic life varied tremendously between the royal homes of the 'Widow of Windsor', the suburban detached villa of a middle class tradesman and the terraced houses of the urban working class. It is pointless to generalise about large and varied groups in any society, but the royal family did provide a 'model' image which many people felt ought to be followed.

- What do extracts A to D tell us about the attitudes of Prince Albert and Queen Victoria towards their children's upbringing?
- Is there any hint in Victoria's comments to suggest that her attitudes changed as her children grew up? (Her youngest child, Beatrice, was born in 1857.)
- What does Kipling's verse tell us about his view of Victoria and her 'Sons'? Does it add anything to our understanding of the Queen's attitude to children?
- How useful are these sources in giving us an understanding of family life in Victorian Britain?

THINK ABOUT Family life today.

- Do you think modern society holds the same family ideals as Victorian society?
- How have the roles of mothers, fathers and children changed?

HEART OF THE EMPIRE

The Royal Family

Source A

'It is indeed a pity that you find no consolation in the company of your children. The root of the trouble lies in the mistaken notion that the function of a mother is to be always correcting, scolding, ordering them about...It is not possible to be on happy friendly terms with people you have just been scolding.'

Prince Albert to Queen Victoria, 1856

Source B

'A little after 8...he came in to tell me to get up...little Beatrice used to be so delighted to see him dress...(At meals) he sat at the top of the table and kept us all enlivened by his interesting conversation...The younger children he kept in order if they ate badly or untidily...He could not bear bad manners and always dealt out his dear reprimands to the juveniles and a word from him was instantly obeyed.'

Queen Victoria describing her late husband, 1862

Source C

'You are wrong in thinking that I am not fond of children. I am. I admire pretty ones especially, pleasant children immensely but I can't bear their being idolised...or having a number of them about me, making a great noise.'

Queen Victoria, 1870

Source D

'For a woman alone to be head of so large a family and at the same time reigning Sovereign is...almost more than human strength can bear...I feel so disheartened. I should like to retire quietly to a cottage in the hills.'

Queen Victoria, 1872

Source E

'Children are a bitter disappointment. Their greatest object being to do precisely what their parents do not wish...often when children have been less watched and less taken care of, the better they turn out! This is...very annoying.'

Queen Victoria, 1876

Source F

'Walk wide o' the Widow at Windsor,
For 'alf o' Creation she owns:
We 'ave bought 'er the same with the sword an' the flame, An' we've salted it down with our bones...
Then 'ere's to the Sons o' the Widow,
Wherever, 'owever they roam.
'Ere's all they desire, an' if they require
A speedy return to their 'ome.'

Rudyard Kipling

This page may be photocopied for classroom use only

THE NATIONAL CURRICULUM

A matrix is provided below in order that teachers may identify where *Britain 1750-1900* and this accompanying teacher-resource book fulfil Attainment Targets of the National Curriculum. The individuals levels are specified in the Resource Book matrix.

	AT1	AT2	AT3
Britain 1750-1900 1	●		
2	●		
3			●
4	●		
5	●		
6	●		
7	●		●
8		●	●
9	●		
10	●		
11	●		
12	●		
13	●		
14	●		
15	●		
16		●	
17	●		
18	●		
19	●		
20	●		●
21	●		●
22	●		●
23	●		●
24	●		●
25	●		●

	AT1	AT2	AT3
Resource Book 1	6c, 7c	7	
2	7a		
3			1, 2, 3
4			1, 2, 3, 5
5	6c		
6	2c, 6c, 8b		
7			3, 4
8			4, 5, 6
9	2a, 3c, 5c		
10	4a, 5a, 6c		7
11	6c	8, 9	
12	5b, 6c		3
13	6c, 7b		
14		6	
15		3, 6, 7	3, 6
16	2c, 4b		
17	7c		4
18			3
19	3a, 6c, 7a		
20	6c, 7c, 9b		
21	2c, 3b		
22	6c		5

Solutions to the exercise in Unit 2:

1 = The *City of Paris* 1888
2 = The *Britannia* 1840
3 = The *Great Britain* 1843
4 = The *East Indiaman* 1760

5 = The *Turbinia* 1897
6 = The *Great Eastern* 1857
7 = Warship 1865
8 = Tea Clipper 1860